DISCERNMENT

LIVING
THE GOOD LIFE
TOGETHER

DISCERNMENT
acting wisely

leader guide

Helen R. Neinast

ABINGDON PRESS / Nashville

LIVING THE GOOD LIFE TOGETHER
DISCERNMENT: ACTING WISELY
Leader Guide

Copyright © 2007 by Abingdon Press

Scripture quotations in this publication, unless otherwise indicated, are from the New Revised Standard Version of the Bible, copyrighted © 1989 by the Division of Christian Education of the National Council of the Churches of Christ in the United States of America, and are used by permission.

Lectio divina steps adapted by permission from *50 Ways to Pray: Practices From Many Traditions and Times*, by Teresa A. Blythe (Abingdon Press, 2006); pages 45–47.

This book is printed on acid-free, elemental chlorine-free paper.

ISBN 978-0-687-64334-9

07 08 09 10 11 12 13 14 15 16—10 9 8 7 6 5 4 3 2 1
MANUFACTURED IN THE UNITED STATES OF AMERICA

Contents

Session Plans

Additional Helps

Introduction

LIVING THE GOOD LIFE TOGETHER: A STUDY OF CHRISTIAN CHARACTER IN COMMUNITY

Welcome to Living the Good Life Together! This unique and exciting series is designed to help Christians learn about and put into practice various character traits associated with the Christian faith. Some of these character traits are attentiveness, forgiveness, discernment, intimacy, humility, and hospitality.

Christian life invites us to cultivate habits that continually open us and others to God's grace, a grace that reshapes our desires, thoughts, feelings, and actions. The "good life" in Christ is life shaped by God's grace. When we choose to seek this good life together, we are drawn into the disciplined habits of living as friends of God in the community of others.

Jesus' ministry was spent teaching and showing others God's good life, so much so that he invested extraordinary time and energy with his disciples. In John 1:39, Jesus invited would-be followers to "come and see." This is a response that facilitates learning and understanding. Luke 10:37 offers Jesus' instruction to "go and do likewise," the closing words to the parable of the good Samaritan. With these words, Jesus invites listeners to practice what they have learned about compassion and mercy, to go and do what is neighborly.

Learning about and practicing the character traits of the Christian life can be compared to learning how to play the piano. We must learn basics such as the position of our hands, the scales, how to use the foot pedals, rhythm, melody, and note reading. If we practice, our skill improves. We are able to play music for others as well as for ourselves. And we find joy in the music!

In a similar way, Living the Good Life Together is designed to help us practice being Christian. Each unit is intended to help us understand or learn about an aspect of Christian character, then move into the practice of what we have learned. Together we will explore and practice ways to embody Christian character in community. And we will find joy in the good life!

A billboard or bumper sticker would say it more succinctly: "The Good Life: Get It. Try It. Live It—Together."

DISCERNMENT: ACTING WISELY

Discernment is the Christian character trait featured in this study of Living the Good Life Together. The writer defines *discernment* as seeking God with all our senses—taste, sight, sound, smell, and touch. It means using all our senses to discern the presence of God—and to do this with clarity. Such discernment informs wise actions in our daily lives.

Our study of discernment will be far ranging. Discernment is critical when it comes to something as daunting as putting a country back together after years of great violence. Desmond Tutu, writing of South Africa's struggle to recover from apartheid, refers time and again to the hard work of discernment. But putting a single life back together after tragedy has taken its toll also demands great compassion and careful discernment. Wisdom gained through discernment is critical in both situations.

Discernment is about big things, about life-changing events and decisions. But discernment is also about everyday things. In which direction do you set your feet in the morning? How open is your heart to the gift of birds and trees and song? How does the pace of life you keep each week allow small acts of compassion and kindness?

In great things, in small things, God calls us to discern God's presence. Sometimes discernment comes quickly, with inspiration and sure knowing. Other times, it comes slowly, painstakingly, and even seemingly not at all.

The Bible is the story of God's people's attempts to be faithful by discerning God's presence in their faith community and in their individual lives. Sometimes these stories are full of irony and almost comical. Sometimes they are dead earnest, filled with tears and struggle. But always, God's promise to be with us—in clarity and in confusion—is true. We are not left to ourselves alone. The challenge of the faith is to discern, to understand just where God is, even when we don't feel God's presence, and then to act with faith in God's presence.

This study is an opportunity to learn about discernment in the Scriptures, and to discover how to seek and discern God's presence in our lives, our work, and our world. This study is about learning how to discern so that we may learn how to join God in the work and world where God is. "Discerning God's Presence in Our Midst" invites us to take a close look at our daily lives and find God close around us. "Discerning God's Presence in Our Work" explores work as something done—with discernment—for the common good. "Discerning God's Presence in the Shadows" examines what it means, as a person of faith to experience the absence of God, and to be able to adjust our seeing so that we may be ready to recognize God's presence. "Discerning God's Presence in Our Habit of Being" encourages us to carry the practice of discernment so closely that we carry our awareness of God with us wherever we are and that we act out of that awareness. "Planning the Next Steps Together" facilitates a group planning process for putting into practice what the group has learned about discernment. All the sessions help to us deepen our relationship with God and to practice discernment as a spiritual discipline.

Resource Components

The resources and group sessions in this study function together to foster intimacy with Scripture, with God, and with others. The resources include a study & reflection guide for each participant, a DVD for viewing during group sessions, and this leader guide.

Study & Reflection Guide

The study & reflection guide is designed for use by the group participants. Each person in the group should have his or her own copy. This guide contains the core content of the study. It also contains several important features in addition to the core content.

Psalm for Praying

A psalm appears on the first page of each session. The group will use this psalm as a prayer of invocation at the beginning of the session.

Daily Readings

Scripture readings are included for each day of the week between the group sessions. Participants will read and reflect upon these Scriptures and use the space provided to write notes or questions they would like to bring to the group session. You will also do these daily readings.

Reflections

When introducing core content, space is provided at the bottom of the page for making notes or recording any thoughts brought to mind by the readings.

Faithful Friends

Each participant will be invited to join with one or two others to practice being a faithful friend over the course of the study and beyond. Spaces are provided at the end of Sessions 2–5 in the study & reflection guide where participants can record thoughts, reflections, insights, prayer concerns, or other matters concerning their faithful friends.

DVD

The video segments on the DVD are designed to supplement the core content presented in the study & reflection guide and to inspire and invite the group into the practice of a particular aspect of Christian character. These segments are 6–10 minutes long and will be viewed during the group sessions, as described in this leader guide.

Leader Guide

The leader guide is designed to help you lead your group with confidence and inspiration. It contains all the information you need in order to help your group plan and carry out the study.

Besides introducing the series and the topic of this particular study, the leader guide also provides detailed session plans. These session plans give you easy-to-follow instructions, including what materials you will need and how to prepare the learning area. The plans also encourage you to set aside a time of preparation before the actual session to prepare yourself spiritually and review your approach to the session.

The leader guide introduces you to the unique "Come and See/Go and Do" format of the study, including additional helps and examples to use as you implement that format. The leader guide concludes with suggestions for planning a final worship and celebration experience.

STUDY FORMAT

The format of this study series is based on some of Jesus' own words to his followers: "Come and see" (John 1:39), and "Go and do likewise" (Luke 10:37). In each study, the first six sessions are the backbone of the "Come and See" portion. These sessions inspire and teach the group about a particular character trait of the Christian life. The second six sessions are the "Go and Do" portion. For these sessions, the study offers tools to help group members plan how to put into practice what they have learned.

"Come and See"

Session 1: An Introduction to This Study Series

This session is an orientation to the twelve-week study. In the session, group members will learn about the series, the study format, and the particular topic of this study. They will become familiar with the study & reflection guide and learn about the video presentations. They will learn about the term *faithful friends* and about the practice of *lectio divina*.

Sessions 2–5: Topics in Christian Character

These sessions offer information about the Christian character trait explored in this particular study. The sessions have a format designed to teach participants about the character trait and to foster intimacy with Scripture, with others, and with God.

Session 6: Planning the Next Steps Together

This session facilitates planning for what the group will do together in Sessions 7–12 to practice the Christian character trait they have learned about in the previous sessions. Session 6 in this leader guide, "Planning the Next Steps Together," offers a flexible, step-by-step guide for leading the group through the planning process.

The session builds upon a brainstorming activity that the participants will do before they come together. The participants will write their ideas where prompted in the study & reflection guide before coming to Session 6. Make sure they understand the importance of doing this brainstorming activity ahead of time.

"Go and Do"

Sessions 7–12: Practicing Christian Character

What will the group do?

These "Go and Do" sessions are meant to allow time to live out some of what the group has learned in the "Come and See" portion of the study. The group will put into practice what they planned during Session 6, "Planning the Next Steps Together." The group will also continue the practice of faithful friends throughout this portion of the study.

The group may use these sessions in any number of ways. The idea is to reinforce what they have learned and to deepen their practice of the particular aspect of Christian character. The group might consider planning activities in some of the following categories, which are also given as prompts in the study & reflection guide:

- Lectio divina Scripture passages
- Behavioral changes to make
- Ministry events to consider

- Mission work to conceive and implement
- Speakers to invite
- Field trips, retreats, pilgrimages to take
- Books to read, movies to see

Possibilities for these next sessions can be varied and creative. There are many movies that lend themselves to group study. You could borrow these from your church or a public library or rent them from a video store. Watch these together and discuss. This is a good way to learn more about those in your group as well as about yourself. Is there a book the group could read and discuss together? a series of audio programs? Is there someone in your church or community you would like to invite to share the group's time together? What about additional Bible study? Would each group member want to bring in something—an article, a story, something found on the Internet—for the group to discuss from week to week?

How often will the group meet?

The group will decide how many times and on what dates they will meet. Your group may want to continue meeting weekly, or they may decide meeting dates based upon the types of activities they choose to do. A retreat, for example, may involve an overnight gathering. A mission experience could involve one day or several days. A book study might involve two or more weekly sessions. The point is to plan activities that the group will do together in order to put into practice what they have learned; then, let the content of what you have planned dictate and shape the frequency and format of your meetings.

The final session, which will also be planned by the group, will be a worship and celebration of what the group has learned and practiced during their time together. It will inspire all who have participated in the study to put into everyday life the practices of Christian character they have explored together. It will offer opportunities to express gratitude and commitment to God.

(See ideas for this worship and celebration in the "Additional Helps" section on pages 57–62.)

Session Activities

During Sessions 1–6, the "Come and See" portion of the study, you will lead your group through a regular sequence of activities described in this section. These activities are designed to bring the group together, to create an environment for learning, and to help the group use videos, books, Scripture, and group discussion to explore Christian character. Details of how to prepare for and implement these activities, week by week, are spelled out in this leader guide under "Session Plans" (pages 23–55).

During Sessions 7–12, the "Go and Do" portion of the study, your group will be following its own session plans, but you may want to continue some of the following activities as a part of those sessions.

Welcome

Greet participants, especially members who are new to the study. Remind them to use nametags, and make them feel welcome.

Psalm and Silence

In the "Come and See" sessions, Psalm and Silence is a time to center as a group using the psalms provided on the opening page of each session in the study & reflection guide. For the "Go and Do" sessions, you may choose other psalms, Scripture passages, or readings.

Look and Listen

The group will view the video segments as described in the session plans. For later sessions, your group can use any other materials they choose, such as books, movies, Scripture passages, and group members' experiences.

Reflect and Respond

This is a time to reflect upon and respond to the content of the particular session. Allow for discussion, dialogue, and questions from everyone in the group.

Lectio Divina

The group will experience the ancient practice of prayerfully reading the Scriptures. The practice is described, step by step, in both the study & reflection guide and the leader guide (see following).

Pray and Practice

This is a time for closing reflections—about the material, about faithful friend experiences, or about prayer concerns. Close this session with prayer in any way your group wishes.

LECTIO DIVINA

Lectio divina, which means "sacred reading," is also called "praying the Scriptures." It is an ancient process for engaging the Scriptures in order to hear the voice of God. Sessions 1–5 of the study include lectio divina for a particular Scripture related to the topic of the session. Groups may choose to incorporate the practice of lectio divina in later sessions as well.

The lectio divina process contains the following steps:

Step One: *Silencio*

After everyone has turned to the Scripture, be still. Silently turn all your thoughts and desires over to God. Let go of concerns, worries, or agendas. Just *be* for a few minutes.

Step Two: *Lectio*

Read the short passage of Scripture slowly and carefully, either aloud or silently. Reread it. Be alert to any word, phrase, or image that invites you, that puzzles you, that intrigues you. Wait for this word, phrase, or image to come to you; try not to rush it.

Step Three: *Meditatio*

Take the word, phrase, or image from your Scripture passage that comes to you and ruminate over it. Repeat it to yourself. Allow this word, phrase, or image to engage your thoughts, your desires, your memories. Invite anyone who would like to share his or her word, phrase, or image, but don't pressure anyone to speak.

Step Four: *Oratio*

Pray that God transform you through the word, phrase, or image from Scripture. Consider how this word, phrase, or image connects with your life and how God is made known to you in it. This prayer may be either silent or spoken.

Step Five: *Contemplatio*

Rest silently in the presence of God. Move beyond words, phrases, or images. Again, just *be* for a few minutes. Close this time of lectio divina with "Amen."

The preceding steps are also listed in each session plan. Participants will find them in the study & reflection guide on pages 12–13.

FAITHFUL FRIENDS

Each week, pairs or small groups of faithful friends will get together to talk about their experience of practicing the week's discipline. Developing and nurturing faithful friends are important practices that continue throughout the twelve weeks of the study. The Christian way of life presupposes healthy relationships with God, self, and neighbor in Christ. Learning how to give and to receive the support of a faithful friend is a cornerstone of living the good life together.

The spiritual discipline of faithful friendship may be uncomfortable for some in the group. Some people are quiet and introspective, and the thought of talking about deep, heartfelt issues of Christian faith may feel threatening to them. For this reason, it is important to give a great deal of freedom to the participants in choosing faithful friends and deciding how they wish to support one another during the weeks of the study. The following questions can ease faithful friends into conversation in a nonthreatening way.

Faithful friends can stay in touch by e-mail, telephone, or over lunch or coffee. They may think of other ways to stay in touch, such as visiting one another in their homes or enjoying a recreational activity together. In these kinds of activities, encourage participants to take time to talk about the study.

Some faithful friends will appreciate guidance for their conversations together. Encourage them to use the following questions, which are also listed on page 14 in the study & reflection guide.

- How has it gone for you, trying to live the week's practice?
- What's been hard about it?
- What's been easy or comfortable?
- What challenges have there been? What rewards?
- What kinds of things happened this week—at work, at home, in your prayer life—that you want to talk about? Has anything affected your spiritual life and walk?

Faithful friends may meet or communicate as often as they like. The expectation is that they communicate at least once a week. During each session, ask the group as a whole how the practice of faithful friends is going. Ask how they are choosing to communicate. Remind them that faithful friends provide a rewarding way to experience meaningful spiritual growth. Also remind them that they can record any thoughts, reflections, insights, prayer concerns, or other matters concerning their faithful friends in the spaces provided in their study & reflection guide (Sessions 2–5).

Do not ask individual participants to talk about their faithful friends conversations. Doing so may cause embarrassment or unnecessary pressure. As a leader, your comments about the practice of having faithful friends should be supportive and affirming.

If the faithful friends practice does not seem to be going well for some of the participants, do not criticize them. Simply suggest a phone call, card, or e-mail saying they are thinking about the faithful friend or praying for them. Every day is a new day that offers many opportunities to support one another. Remind participants to honor confidentiality with their faithful friends, to pray for their faithful friends and for their own role as a faithful friend, to listen deeply to one another, and to demonstrate respect for one another.

How to Organize a Group

Living the Good Life Together is an excellent resource for all people who are looking for meaning in their daily lives, who want to grow in their faith, and who want to practice specific traits of Christian character. Group members may be persons who are not a part of a faith community and yet are seekers on a profound spiritual journey. They may be new Christians or new church members who want to know more about Christian faith. Or they may be people who have been in church a long time but feel a need for spiritual renewal. All such persons desire to engage more deeply with what it means to practice the Christian faith.

In order to start a Living the Good Life Together group, you may want to follow these steps:

1. Read through the leader guide and the study & reflection guide. View all the video segments on the DVD. Think about the specific character trait dealt with in the study, the issues it generates, and the Scriptures. Prepare to respond to questions that someone may ask about the study.

2. Develop a list of potential group members. An ideal size for a small group is seven to twelve people. Your list should have about twice your target number (fourteen to twenty-four people). Encourage your local church to purchase a copy of the study & reflection guide for each of the persons on your list. This is an invaluable outreach tool.

3. Decide on a location and time for your group.

4. Identify someone who is willing to go with you to visit the persons on your list. Make it your goal to become acquainted with each person you visit. Tell them about Living the Good Life Together. Give them a copy of the study & reflection guide. Even if they choose not to attend the group at this time, they will have an opportunity to study the book on their own. Tell each person the initial meeting time, location, and how many weeks the group will meet. Invite them to become a part of the group. Thank them for their time.

5. Publicize the study through as many channels as are available. Announce it during worship. Print notices in the church newsletter and bulletin and on the church website if you have one. Use free public-event notices in community newspapers. Create fliers for mailing and posting in public places.

6. A few days before the sessions begin, give a friendly phone call or send an e-mail to thank all persons you visited for their consideration and interest. Remind them of the time and location of the first meeting.

How to Lead a Group

The role of the leader is to use the resources and facilitate the group sessions in order to foster intimacy with Scripture, with God, and with others. So what does a leader do?

A Leader Prepares

This leader guide contains specific instructions for planning and implementing the study. Generally speaking, however, a leader has some basic preparation responsibilities. They are:

Pray

Ask for God's guidance as you prepare to lead the session.

Read

Review the session materials and its Scriptures ahead of time. Jot down questions or insights that occur during the reading.

Think About Group Participants

Who are they? What life issues or questions might they have about the theme? about the Scriptures?

Prepare the Learning Area

Gather any needed supplies, such as large sheets of paper, markers, paper and pencils, Bibles, hymn books, audiovisual equipment, masking tape, a Bible dictionary, or Bible commentaries. If you are meeting in a classroom setting, arrange the chairs in a semicircle so that everyone can easily see the video segments that will be shown during the session. Make sure everyone will have a place to sit.

Pray for the Group Participants

Before the participants arrive, pray for each one. Ask for God's blessing on your session. Offer thanks to God for the opportunity to lead the session.

A Leader Creates a Welcoming Atmosphere

Hospitality is a spiritual discipline. A leader helps to create an environment that makes others feel welcome and helps every participant experience the freedom to ask questions and to state opinions. Such an atmosphere is based upon mutual respect.

Greet Participants as They Arrive

Say aloud the name of each participant. If the class is meeting for the first time, use nametags.

Listen

As group discussion unfolds, affirm the comments and ideas of participants. Avoid the temptation to dominate conversation or "correct" the ideas of participants.

Affirm

Thank people for telling about what they think or feel. Acknowledge their contributions to discussion in positive ways, even if you disagree with their ideas.

A Leader Facilitates Discussion

Ask Questions

Use the questions suggested in the session plans or other questions that occur to you as you prepare for the session. Encourage others to ask questions.

Invite Silent Participants to Contribute Ideas

If someone in the group is quiet, you might say something like, "I'm interested in what you're thinking." If participants seem hesitant or shy, do not pressure them to speak. However, do communicate your interest.

Gently Redirect Discussion When Someone in the Group Dominates

You can do this in several ways. Remind the group as a whole that everyone's ideas are important. Invite them to respect one another and to allow others the opportunity to express their ideas. You may establish a group covenant that clarifies such mutual respect. Use structured methods such as going around the circle to allow everyone a chance to speak. Only as a last resort, speak to the person who dominates conversation after the group meeting.

Session Plans

1. AN INTRODUCTION TO THIS STUDY SERIES

Prepare for the Session

Let your preparation for the session be a time to pay attention to God and to the needs of group members as well as a time to review the content of the session. Find a quiet and comfortable place where you will not be interrupted. Have the DVD, a Bible, and the study & reflection guide available in addition to this leader guide. Have paper and pen available to jot down notes or insights. You may wish to keep these notes in a personal journal during this study.

Pray, asking for God's guidance as you prepare for the session. Read Psalm 1:1-3. Take a moment to reflect upon how this Scripture speaks to you.

Review the information about Living the Good Life Together in the introduction to the leader guide to make sure you understand the process for the sessions in the series. Anticipate questions group members might have about the program. Write down any notes and questions you have.

View the video segments "Series Overview" and "*Come and See: Preview.*" Write notes and questions suggested by the video segments. If you have time, view all the video segments in the study in order to have a more complete overview.

Read the introduction to the series in the study & reflection guide. Write notes and questions suggested by the material.

Review the information about lectio divina in the introduction to this leader guide (pages 16–17). Read Isaiah 11:1-3 using this process. Write notes or questions that emerge from your reading. Consider what this Scripture says to you about the relationship of discernment and acting wisely.

Review the information about faithful friends in the introduction to this leader guide and in the following instructions. Make sure you understand the purpose and process for this practice. Consider ways to support and encourage the process for the group members.

Review the steps in "Lead the Session."

Pray, offering gratitude to God for insights, ideas, and guidance for the session. Give thanks for the group members and for what you will experience together.

Gather Materials and Set Up the Learning Area

- Bibles
- DVD, DVD player, and TV
- Leader guide
- Study & reflection guides, one for each participant
- Nametags and markers or pens
- Chairs in a semicircle for viewing the video

Lead the Session

Welcome (3 minutes)

Greet participants as they arrive. Invite them to make a nametag and to find a place to sit where they can comfortably view the video.

Psalm and Silence (3 minutes)

A psalm for praying appears on the first page of each session of the study & reflection guide. This session is "An Introduction to This Study Series," so participants will not yet have the printed material in front of them for the psalm. Read Psalm 1:1-3 as a prayer of invocation. Follow the praying of the psalm with at least a minute of silence.

Look and Listen (8 minutes)

Introduce the first video segment as follows: "This video presentation offers an overview of our study of Living the Good Life Together. It will invite us to consider the Christian character trait of intimacy." Then view the video segment "Series Overview."

Reflect and Respond (5 minutes)

Following the video, lead the group in discussing the following questions:
- Whom did you recognize in the photographs at the beginning of the video? What thoughts or feelings did these images evoke for you?
- Learning to play the piano illustrates the need to practice in order to learn a skill. What do you remember about learning a new skill? How does this experience connect to learning to live as a Christian?

Overview of Living the Good Life Together (8 minutes)

Tell About the Study Format

Tell the group members about how Living the Good Life Together will work. The total time for the study is twelve weeks. The structure of the study is based upon Jesus' words to the disciples. The first six sessions, "Come and See," will focus on learning and understanding.

Read aloud John 1:38-39. Tell the group that the "Come and See" part of the study is based upon this Scripture.

The second six sessions, "Go and Do," will focus on application or practice. Read aloud Luke 10:36-37, the end of the parable of the good Samaritan. Tell the group that the "Go and Do" part of the study is based upon this Scripture.

Session 6 of the "Come and See" part will be a group planning time for Sessions 7–12. The group will make plans for "Go and Do" based upon what they have learned in "Come and See." Session 12 will conclude with a worship and celebration for the study on forgiveness.

Tell About the Study & Reflection Guide

Give each participant a study & reflection guide. Tell them to turn to pages 11–12. Together, look at the section describing the study & reflection guide. Read aloud the paragraphs entitled "Psalm for Praying," "Daily Readings," and "Reflections."

Tell About the Video Segments

Tell participants that the group sessions will include a brief video segment designed to inspire and to invite reflection and discussion about forgiveness. The video segments supplement and enhance the core content presented in the study & reflection guide.

Faithful Friends (5 minutes)

Ask the group to look at the section on faithful friends on pages 13–14 of the study & reflection guide. You may say something like the following:

- Pairs or small groups of faithful friends will get together during the week to talk about their experiences with the study. This might be over lunch or coffee, during a walk, or by phone or e-mail.
- Use the following questions to help start your conversation:
  - ✓ How has it gone for you, trying to live the week's practice?
  - ✓ What's been hard about it?
  - ✓ What's been easy or comfortable?
  - ✓ What challenges have there been? What rewards?
  - ✓ What kinds of things happened this week—at work, at home, in your prayer life—that you want to talk about? Has anything affected your spiritual life and walk?
- Ask group members to find a partner or partners. You may ask people to pair up on their own, or you may have people number off to get into pairs. If the group has an odd number of people, ask one group to form as three. Be sure to include yourself in this process of forming faithful friends. Tell the group there will be suggestions at the end of today's session for what they might do this week as faithful friends.

Overview of DISCERNMENT: ACTING WISELY *(5 minutes)*

Ask participants to look on pages 14–16 in the study & reflection guide at the section called "Discernment: Acting Wisely." Share in your own words the information from the introduction to this leader guide under "Discernment: Acting Wisely" (pages 8–10). Emphasize the following points from this material:

- Discernment is about big things—life-changing events and decisions. Discernment is also about small things—the way you

27

live your life every day, how your actions determine who you are, how you seek God moment-to-moment and day-to-day.

- Sometimes discernment comes quickly, with inspiration and sure knowing. Other times, the process of discernment can be slow, painstaking, and frustrating.
- The Bible is the story of people who tried to be faithful and to discern who God wanted them to be, as a community and as individuals.
- Whether seeking God brings clarity or confusion, God's promise to be with us in the seeking life is strong, sure, and trustworthy. No matter where we wander in our faith lives, God will be there.
- We learn how to discern so that we may learn how to act wisely, that is, how to join God in the work and the world where God is.

Lectio Divina (10 minutes)

For this introductory session, the group will not have read any Bible passages or chapter content. Invite someone to read aloud Isaiah 11:1-3. Ask what this Scripture means in light of the theme of discernment and acting wisely.

Tell the group that they will use the ancient practice of lectio divina to prayerfully engage Isaiah 11:1-3. As a group, use the lectio divina approach outlined as follows to pray this Scripture.

Step One: *Silencio*

After everyone has turned to the Scripture, be still. Silently turn all your thoughts and desires over to God. Let go of concerns, worries, or agendas. Just *be* for a few minutes.

Step Two: *Lectio*

Read the short passage of Scripture slowly and carefully, either aloud or silently. Reread it. Be alert to any word, phrase, or image that invites you, that puzzles you, that intrigues you. Wait for this word, phrase, or image to come to you; try not to rush it.

Step Three: *Meditatio*

Take the word, phrase, or image from your Scripture passage that comes to you and ruminate over it. Repeat it to yourself. Allow this word, phrase, or image to engage your thoughts, your desires, your memories. Invite anyone who would like to share his or her word, phrase, or image, but don't pressure anyone to speak.

Step Four: *Oratio*

Pray that God transform you through the word, phrase, or image from Scripture. Consider how this word, phrase, or image connects with your life and how God is made known to you in it. This prayer may be either silent or spoken.

Step Five: *Contemplatio*

Rest silently in the presence of God. Move beyond words, phrases, or images. Again, just *be* for a few minutes. Close this time of lectio divina with "Amen."

Look and Listen (6 minutes)

Introduce the second video segment as follows: "This video presentation offers a preview of our study of discernment. It will invite us to consider the spiritual discipline of discernment, that is, seeking God and acting wisely in our lives." Then view the video segment "*Come and See*. Preview."

Pray and Practice (5 minutes)

This Week's Practice

Encourage group members to do the following:

- Contact their faithful friend this week for coffee, lunch, a walk, or a phone conversation, and talk with that friend about her or his experience of practicing intimacy this week. Remind the friend to use the list of questions in the "Faithful Friends" section of Session 1, "An Introduction to This Study Series," in the study & reflection guide (pages 13–14).
- Do the daily readings listed in Session 2: "Discerning God's Presence in Our Midst" in the study & reflection guide (pages 18–19).
- In the study & reflection guide, review Session 1, "An Introduction to This Study Series." Then read Session 2, "Discerning God's Presence in Our Midst" (pages 20–24). Write notes or questions for discussion in the reflections space. Invite them to consider the relationship of discernment and acting wisely as they write their notes.

Closing Prayer

- Share prayer concerns.
- Invite participants to pray for their faithful friend and for the group this week.
- Imagine and discuss possible steps that group members might take this week to put into practice the week's learnings.

Close with a prayer asking God to support each participant. Pray that group members will sense God's support and the encouragement of the group as they seek ways to practice intimacy during the weeks ahead.

2. DISCERNING GOD'S PRESENCE IN OUR MIDST

Prepare for the Session

Let your preparation for the session be a time to pay attention to God and to the needs of group members as well as a time to review the content of the session. Find a quiet and comfortable place where you will not be interrupted. Have the DVD, a Bible, and the study & reflection guide available in addition to this leader guide. Have paper and pen available to jot down notes or insights.

Pray, asking God's guidance as you prepare for the session. Read Psalm 8:1, 3-6, 9 prayerfully.

View the video segment "Discerning God's Presence in Our Midst." Write notes and questions suggested by the video.

Read Session 2, "Discerning God's Presence in Our Midst," in the study & reflection guide and the Scriptures mentioned in the daily readings and text. Write notes and questions suggested by the material. Consider ways the Scriptures and the chapter material relate to discernment and to acting wisely.

Review the description of lectio divina in the introduction to this leader guide (pages 16–17). Read 1 Kings 4:29-34 using this process. Write notes or questions that emerge from your reading. Consider what 1 Kings 4:29-34 says about the relationship of wisdom, discernment, and acting wisely.

Review the steps in "Lead the Session."

Pray, offering gratitude to God for insights, ideas, and guidance during the session. Thank God for the group members and for what you will experience together.

Gather Materials and Set Up the Learning Area

- Bibles
- DVD, DVD player, and TV
- Leader guide

- Study & reflection guide, one for each participant (participants may bring their own copies)
- Nametags and markers or pens
- Chairs in a semicircle for viewing the video

Lead the Session

Welcome (5 minutes)

Greet participants as they arrive. Invite them to take a nametag and find a place to sit where they can comfortably view the video.

Psalm and Silence (3 minutes)

Read Psalm 8:1, 3-6, 9 as a prayer of invocation. Follow the praying of the psalm with at least a minute of silence.

Look and Listen (10 minutes)

Introduce the video segment as follows: "This video presentation will help us explore meanings of discernment." Then view the video segment, "Discerning God's Presence in Our Midst."

Reflect and Respond (25 minutes)

Following the video segment, lead the group in discussing these questions:
- Which definition of *discernment* resonated most with you? How do you define *discernment*?
- How do you feel about praying for God's wisdom about our small, daily concerns?
- How did you respond to the comparison of discernment to baking bread and to the idea of waiting through the process of discernment?
- What do you think about the description of discernment as an ongoing process that does not end?

Invite participants to recall the daily readings in the Bible done in preparation for the group meeting. Ask:

- What did the Scriptures say to you about discerning God's presence?
- What did the Scriptures say about wisdom and understanding as part of discernment? about acting wisely as a result of discernment?
- Has there been a time in your life when you relied on Luke's admonition to ask, search, or knock? What was the occasion? What feelings or thoughts do you have about the experience?

Invite participants to recall the daily readings in the Bible done in preparation for the group meeting. Ask:

- What thoughts or questions did you write in the spaces for reflection?
- What do you think of Sue Anne Steffey Morrow's hope that we might involve all our senses to discern God's presence (page 23)? Do you recall a time when using a sense other than sight and sound brought you closer to God?
- Consider how you see and discern God in the midst of your daily life. For example, is it in the smell of your grandmother's cookies, the memory of a five-year-old helping a friend who has fallen down, in the study of the Bible, the song of a thrush in the woods, or in another similar occasion? What difference does such discernment make in your daily actions?

Lectio Divina (10 minutes)

As a group, use the approach outlined as follows to pray this Scripture: 1 Kings 4:29-34.

Step One: *Silencio*

After everyone has turned to the Scripture, be still. Silently turn all your thoughts and desires over to God. Let go of concerns, worries, or agendas. Just *be* for a few minutes.

Step Two: *Lectio*

Read the short passage of Scripture slowly and carefully, either aloud or silently. Reread it. Be alert to any word, phrase, or image that invites you, that puzzles you, that intrigues you. Wait for this word, phrase, or image to come to you; try not to rush it.

Step Three: *Meditatio*

Take the word, phrase, or image that comes to you from your Scripture passage and ruminate over it. Repeat it to yourself. Allow this word, phrase, or image to engage your thoughts, your desires, your memories. Invite anyone who would like to share his or her word, phrase, or image, but do not pressure anyone to speak.

Step Four: *Oratio*

Pray that God transform you through the word, phrase, or image from Scripture. Consider how this word, phrase, or image connects with your life and how God is made known to you in it. This prayer may be either silent or spoken.

Step Five: *Contemplatio*

Rest silently in the presence of God. Move beyond words, phrases, or images. Again, just *be* for a few minutes. Close this time of lectio divina with "Amen."

Pray and Practice (5 minutes)

This Week's Practice

Encourage group members to do the following:
• Contact their faithful friend this week and talk with that friend about his or her experience in the practice of discernment. Remind them to use the list of questions in the "Faithful Friends" section of Session 1, "An Introduction to This Study Series," in the study & reflection guide (pages 13–14).

- Do the daily readings listed in Session 3, "Discerning God's Presence in Our Work" in the study & reflection guide (pages 28–29).
- Read Session 3, "Discerning God's Presence in Our Work" in the study & reflection guide (pages 30–34). Write notes or questions for reflection or discussion in the reflections space.

Closing Prayer

- Share prayer concerns.
- Invite participants to pray this week for their faithful friend and for the group.
- Imagine and discuss possible steps that group members might take to put into practice the week's learnings about discernment, God's all-encompassing presence, and our call to "look" with all our senses for God's presence in the world. Pray that discernment will inform and encourage acting wisely during the week.

Close with a prayer asking God to support each participant. Pray that group members will sense God's support and the encouragement of the group as they think about what it means to live in God's presence and to be open to discerning God's presence in our midst.

3. DISCERNING GOD'S PRESENCE IN OUR WORK

Prepare for the Session

Let your preparation for the session be a time to pay attention to God and to the needs of group members as well as a time to review the content of the session. Find a quiet and comfortable place where you will not be interrupted. Have the DVD, a Bible, and the study & reflection guide available in addition to this leader guide. Have paper and pen available to jot down notes or insights.

Pray, asking God's guidance as you prepare for the session. Read prayerfully Psalm 86:10-12.

View the video segment "Discerning God's Presence in Our Work." Write notes and questions suggested by the video.

Read Session 3, "Discerning God's Presence in Our Work," in the study & reflection guide and the Scriptures mentioned in the daily readings and text. Write notes and questions suggested by the material.

Review the description of lectio divina in the introduction to this leader guide (pages 16–17). Read Proverbs 31:10-31 using this process. Write notes or questions that emerge from your reading.

Review the steps in "Lead the Session."

Pray, offering gratitude to God for insights, ideas, and guidance for the session. Thank God for the group members and for what you will experience together.

Gather Materials and Set Up the Learning Area

- Bibles
- DVD, DVD player, and TV
- Leader guide
- Study & reflection guide, one for each participant (participants may bring their own copies)
- Nametags and markers or pens
- Chairs in a semicircle for viewing the video

Lead the Session

Welcome (5 minutes)

Greet participants as they arrive. Invite them to take a name-tag and to find a place to sit where they can comfortably view the video.

Psalm and Silence (3 minutes)

Read Psalm 86:10-12 as a prayer of invocation. Follow the praying of the psalm with at least a minute of silence.

Look and Listen (10 minutes)

Introduce the video segment as follows: "This video presentation will help us explore how discernment can help us in our daily work." Then view the video segment, "Discerning God's Presence in Our Work."

Reflect and Respond (25 minutes)

Following the video, lead the group in discussing the following questions:
- How do you feel about the idea that difficult times show that God is testing us?
- When asked how she knew when the dough was ready, the biscuit maker said: "How do I know? I just know!" Have you ever felt like that about discerning God's presence, will, or intention?
- One woman described her journey to discerning her life's work as a series of challenges, changes, and doubts. Have you had an experience similar to hers? What was it like? What do you think about her advice to be willing to accept closed doors or to be willing to simply take the next step?

Invite participants to recall the daily readings in the Bible that were done in preparation for the group meeting. Ask:

- What did the Scriptures say to you about discernment and about acting wisely?
- How did the Scriptures speak to you in regard to discerning God's presence in your work? What difference does the practice of discernment and acting wisely make in your work? Do these reflect discernment of God's presence at work?

Invite participants to recall the session material they read for this week. Ask:

- What thoughts or questions did you write in the reflection spaces?
- How do the voices of residents at Camphill Village speak to you? What connections do you see to the spiritual practice of discernment and acting wisely?
- How do the three threads listed on pages 33–34 speak to you about discernment?
- Donald Hall writes in his essay, "Lifework," that contentment is work so engrossing that you do not know you are working (page 34). He says that hours pass like seconds when work is so absorbing. Have you or someone you know ever experienced this? What was it like? What connections do you make to discernment? The writer asserts that each of us needs work that has meaning and is valued by others. Do you know of people in the world who have no access to meaningful work, or perhaps no access to any work at all? What do you think life is like for these people?

Lectio Divina (10 minutes)

As a group, use the approach outlined as follows to pray this Scripture: Proverbs 31:10-31.

Step One: *Silencio*

After everyone has turned to the Scripture, be still. Silently turn all your thoughts and desires over to God. Let go of concerns, worries, or agendas. Just *be* for a few minutes.

Step Two: *Lectio*

Read the passage of Scripture slowly and carefully, either aloud or silently. Reread it. Be alert to any word, phrase, or image that invites you, that puzzles you, that intrigues you. Wait for this word, phrase, or image to come to you; try not to rush it.

Step Three: *Meditatio*

Take the word, phrase, or image from the Scripture passage that comes to you and ruminate over it. Repeat it to yourself. Allow this word, phrase, or image to engage your thoughts, your desires, your memories. Invite anyone who would like to share his or her word, phrase, or image, but do not pressure anyone to speak.

Step Four: *Oratio*

Pray that God transforms you through the word, phrase, or image from Scripture. Consider how this word, phrase, or image connects with your life and how God is made known to you in it. This prayer may be either silent or spoken.

Step Five: *Contemplatio*

Rest silently in the presence of God. Move beyond words, phrases, or images. Again, just *be* for a few minutes. Close this time of lectio divina with "Amen."

Pray and Practice (5 minutes)

This Week's Practice

Encourage group members to do the following:

- Contact their faithful friend this week. Ask them to talk with their faithful friend about how they might use discernment in their daily work. Remind them to use the list of questions in the "Faithful Friends" section of Session 1, "An Introduction to This Study Series," in the study & reflection guide (pages 13–14).
- Do the daily readings listed in Session 4, "Discerning God's Presence in the Shadows," in the study & reflection guide (pages 38–39). Write notes or questions for reflection or discussion in the reflections space.
- Read Session 4, "Discerning God's Presence in the Shadows," in the study & reflection guide (pages 40–45). Write notes or questions for reflection or discussion in the reflections space.

Closing Prayer

- Share prayer concerns.
- Invite participants to pray for their faithful friend and for the group this week.
- Imagine and discuss possible steps that group members might take to put into practice the week's learnings about discerning God's presence in their work lives and in the work lives of others.

Close with a prayer asking God to support each participant. Pray that God gives group members the courage to discern God's presence in their workplace.

SESSION PLANS

4. DISCERNING GOD'S PRESENCE IN THE SHADOWS

Prepare for the Session

Let your preparation for the session be a time to pay attention to God and to the needs of group members as well as a time to review the content of the session. Find a quiet and comfortable place where you will not be interrupted. Have the DVD, a Bible, and the study & reflection guide available in addition to this leader guide. Have paper and pen available to jot down notes or insights.

Pray, asking God's guidance as you prepare for the session. Read Psalm 42:1-3 prayerfully.

View the video segment "Discerning God's Presence in the Shadows." Write notes and questions suggested by the video.

Read Session 4, "Discerning God's Presence in the Shadows," in the study & reflection guide as well as the Scriptures mentioned in the daily readings and text. Write notes and questions suggested by the material.

Review the description of lectio divina in the introduction to this leader guide (pages 16–17). Read Luke 22:39-44 using this process. Write notes or questions that emerge from your reading.

Review the steps in "Lead the Session."

Pray, offering gratitude to God for insights, ideas, and guidance for the session. Thank God for the group members and for what you will experience together.

Gather Materials and Set Up the Learning Area

- Bibles
- DVD, DVD player, and TV
- Leader guide
- Study & reflection guide, one for each participant (participants may bring their own copies)
- Nametags and markers or pens
- Chairs in a semicircle for viewing the video

41

Lead the Session

Welcome (5 minutes)

Greet participants as they arrive. Invite them to take a name-tag and to find a place to sit where they can comfortably view the video.

Psalm and Silence (3 minutes)

Read Psalm 42:1-3 as a prayer of invocation. Follow the praying of the psalm with at least a minute of silence.

Look and Listen (10 minutes)

Introduce the video segment as follows: "This video presentation explores how discernment can help us experience God's support during difficult times." Then view the video segment "Discerning God's Presence in the Shadows."

Reflect and Respond (25 minutes)

Following the video, lead the group in discussing these questions:
- Have you ever been angry at God or blamed God for your misfortune like the woman who had twins with cancer? What was it like for you? How do you think God was offering you strength through your experience?
- How do you experience God's presence? What do you think of the explanation that like the air around you, you don't have to see God to know God is there?
- The daughter of the Holocaust survivors experienced raindrops as a sign of God's sadness about what had happened at the concentration camp. Have you experienced such signs in your life? What were they and what did they reveal to you about God?

Invite the participants to recall the daily readings in the Bible done in preparation for the group meeting. Ask:
- What did the Scriptures say to you about discernment and acting wisely?
- How did the Scriptures speak to you about discerning God's presence in the shadows, that is, during hard times?
- How do the Scriptures address the sense of God's absence and God's presence in the lives of the faithful?

Invite participants to recall the session material they read for this week. Ask:
- What thoughts or questions did you write in the reflection spaces?
- The author asserts that discerning the presence of God in the shadows is part of what it means to be a Christian. We must adjust our eyes, learn to trust, learn to follow in faith, and hold to the hope that there will come a time when we can turn again toward the light (page 41). Have you experienced such a time in your life? What was that like?
- As disciples, we are called to be the presence of God to one another in dark times (page 43). How does the spiritual practice of discernment prepare us to accompany someone who is living in difficult circumstances?

Lectio Divina (10 minutes)

As a group, use the approach outlined as follows to pray this Scripture: Luke 22:39-44.

Step One: *Silencio*

After everyone has turned to the Scripture, be still. Silently turn all your thoughts and desires over to God. Let go of concerns, worries, or agendas. Just *be* for a few minutes.

Step Two: *Lectio*

Read the short passage of Scripture slowly and carefully, either aloud or silently. Reread it. Be alert to any word, phrase, or image that invites you, that puzzles you, that intrigues you. Wait for this word, phrase, or image to come to you; try not to rush it.

Step Three: *Meditatio*

Take the word, phrase, or image from your Scripture passage that comes to you and ruminate over it. Repeat it to yourself. Allow this word, phrase, or image to engage your thoughts, your desires, your memories. Invite anyone who would like to share his or her word, phrase, or image, but do not pressure anyone to speak.

Step Four: *Oratio*

Pray that God transforms you through the word, phrase, or image from Scripture. Consider how this word, phrase, or image connects with your life and how God is made known to you in it. This prayer may be either silent or spoken.

Step Five: *Contemplatio*

Rest silently in the presence of God. Move beyond words, phrases, or images. Again, just *be* for a few minutes. Close this time of lectio divina with "Amen."

Pray and Practice (5 minutes)

This Week's Practice

Encourage group members to do the following:
- Contact their faithful friend this week. Ask them to talk with their faithful friend about difficult times in their lives when they at first did not recognize God's presence. Remind them to use the list of questions in the "Faithful Friends" section of Session 1, "An Introduction to This Study Series," in the study & reflection guide (pages 13–14).

- Do the daily readings listed in Session 5, "Discerning God's Presence in Our Habit of Being," in the study & reflection guide (pages 48–49).
- Read Session 5, "Discerning God's Presence in Our Habit of Being," in the study & reflection guide (pages 50–55). Write notes or questions for reflection or discussion in the reflections space.

Closing Prayer

- Share prayer concerns.
- Invite participants to pray for their faithful friend and for the group this week.
- Imagine and discuss possible steps that group members might take to prepare themselves for times of discerning God's presence when God seems absent.

Close with a prayer asking God to support each participant. Pray that group members may be able to discern God's presence in good times and in bad.

5. DISCERNING GOD'S PRESENCE IN OUR HABIT OF BEING

Prepare for the Session

Let your preparation for the session be a time to pay attention to God and to the needs of group members as well as a time to review the content of the session. Find a quiet and comfortable place where you will not be interrupted. Have the DVD, a Bible, and the study & reflection guide available in addition to this leader guide. Have paper and pen available to jot down notes or insights.

Pray, asking God's guidance as you prepare for the session. Read prayerfully Psalm 119:33-37.

View the video segment "Discerning God's Presence in Our Habit of Being." Write notes and questions suggested by the video.

Read Session 5, "Discerning God's Presence in Our Habit of Being," in the study & reflection guide and the Scriptures mentioned in the daily readings and text. Write notes and questions suggested by the material.

Review the description of lectio divina in the introduction to this leader guide (pages 16–17). Read Luke 10:25-37 using this process. Write notes or questions that emerge from your reading.

Review the steps in "Lead the Session."

Pray, offering gratitude to God for insights, ideas, and guidance for the session. Thank God for the group members and for what you will experience together.

Gather Materials and Set Up the Learning Area

- Bibles
- DVD, DVD player, and TV
- Leader guide
- Study & reflection guide, one for each participant (participants may bring their own copies)
- Nametags and markers or pens
- Chairs in a semicircle for viewing the video

Lead the Session

Welcome (5 minutes)

Greet participants as they arrive. Invite them to take a name-tag and to find a place to sit where they can comfortably view the video.

Psalm and Silence (3 minutes)

Read Psalm 119:33-37 as a prayer of invocation. Follow the praying of the psalm with at least a minute of silence.

Look and Listen (10 minutes)

Introduce the video segment as follows: "This video presentation challenges us to discern God's will as we reach out to others." Then view the video segment "Discerning God's Presence in Our Habit of Being."

Reflect and Respond (25 minutes)

Following the video, lead the group in discussing these questions:
• What in your daily "habit of being" reflects your identity as God's creation? How do you think that recognition of all people as God's creation can change the way we relate to one another day by day?
• Both the examples of serving the poor and homeless and of helping establish a clinic in Kenya are extraordinary. How do you think we can show God's will and care in the mundane and everyday tasks of life?
• How do you feel about the idea that God is the one who is seeking us more than we are the ones who are seeking God?

Invite the participants to recall the daily readings in the Bible done in preparation for the group meeting. Ask:

- What did the Scriptures say to you about discernment and acting wisely?
- How did the Scriptures speak to you about the call to discern and live God's presence with your "habit of being," that is with your whole life and everything that you do?

Invite participants to recall the session material they read for this week. Ask:

- What thoughts or questions did you write in the reflection spaces?
- The writer writes about the "moral code" embedded in each of the world's major religions (page 51). How would you describe the moral code of Christianity?
- What do you think it means to live within the moral code of a faith community, to come to understand the dimension of holy intention for each of our lives and our life together, and to discern the will of God (page 52)?
- How do you begin to discern the presence of God through your own habit of being? Do the examples of the people mentioned in the study guide help you? Are there other examples that inspire you and draw you closer to God's presence?

Lectio Divina (10 minutes)

As a group, use the approach outlined as follows to pray this Scripture: Luke 10:25-37.

Step One: *Silencio*

After everyone has turned to the Scripture, be still. Silently turn all your thoughts and desires over to God. Let go of concerns, worries, or agendas. Just *be* for a few minutes.

Step Two: *Lectio*

Read the passage of Scripture slowly and carefully, either aloud or silently. Reread it. Be alert to any word, phrase, or image that invites you, that puzzles you, that intrigues you. Wait for this word, phrase, or image to come to you; try not to rush it.

Step Three: *Meditatio*

Take the word, phrase, or image from the Scripture passage that comes to you and ruminate over it. Repeat it to yourself. Allow this word, phrase, or image to engage your thoughts, your desires, your memories. Invite anyone who would like to share his or her word, phrase, or image, but do not pressure anyone to speak.

Step Four: *Oratio*

Pray that God transforms you through the word, phrase, or image from Scripture. Consider how this word, phrase, or image connects with your life and how God is made known to you in it. This prayer may be either silent or spoken.

Step Five: *Contemplatio*

Rest silently in the presence of God. Move beyond words, phrases, or images. Again, just be for a few minutes. Close this time of lectio divina with "Amen."

Pray and Practice (5 minutes)

This Week's Practice

Encourage group members to do the following:
- Contact their faithful friend this week. Ask them to talk with that friend as a resource to strengthen their connection with God. Remind them to use the list of questions in the "Faithful Friends" section of Session 1, "An Introduction to This Study Series," in the study & reflection guide (pages 13–14).
- Read Session 6, "Planning the Next Steps Together," in the study & reflection guide (pages 57–61). Write ideas in the boxes provided (pages 60–61). Remind the group that Session 6 is a planning session for what the group will do together for

the second phase of the study, "Go and Do." The success of Session 6 will depend upon each member of the group brainstorming ideas during the coming week in preparation for the group meeting.

• Continue the practice of lectio divina on their own and with others.

Closing Prayer

• Share prayer concerns.
• Invite participants to pray for their faithful friend and for the group this week.
• Imagine and discuss possible steps that group members might take to put into practice the week's learnings about discernment and the everyday habit of being.

Close with a prayer asking God to support each participant. Pray that group members will be encouraged to seek God's presence in their daily habit of being. Pray for the work group members will do to prepare for the "Go and Do" part of this study on discernment.

6. Planning the Next Steps Together

Prepare for the Session

Let your preparation for the session be a time to pay attention to God and to the needs of group members as well as a time to review the content of the session. Find a quiet and comfortable place where you will not be interrupted. Have the DVD, a Bible, and the study & reflection guide available in addition to this leader guide. Have paper and pen available to jot down notes or insights.

Pray, asking God's guidance as you prepare for the session. Read Psalm 19:7, 9b-10 prayerfully.

Review the information about "Go and Do" in the introduction to this leader guide (pages 13–15) to make sure you understand the planning process for the remaining six sessions. Anticipate questions the group members might have about the program. Write notes and questions you have.

Read Session 6, "Planning the Next Steps Together," in the study & reflection guide (pages 57–61). Write notes and questions suggested by the material. Brainstorm ideas for what you might do as a group over the next six weeks using the idea prompts at the end of the study & reflection guide (pages 60–61).

View the video segment "*Go and Do*: Review and a Challenge." Write notes and questions suggested by the video.

Review the steps in "Lead the Session."

Pray, offering gratitude to God for insights, ideas, and guidance for the session. Thank God for the group members and for what you will experience together.

Gather Materials and Set Up the Learning Area

- Bibles
- DVD, DVD player, and TV
- Leader guide
- Study & reflection guides, one for each participant (participants may bring their own copies)

- Nametags and markers or pens
- Whiteboard and markers, chalkboard and chalk, or a large sheet of paper and markers
- Masking tape
- Pens or pencils
- Chairs arranged in a semicircle for viewing the video

Lead the Session

Welcome (3 minutes)

Greet participants as they arrive. Invite them to find a place to sit where they can comfortably view the video.

Psalm and Silence (5 minutes)

Read Psalm 19:7, 9b-10 as a prayer of invocation. Follow the praying of the psalm with at least a minute of silence.

Look and Listen (8 minutes)

Introduce the video segment as follows: "This video presentation offers a review of what we have studied in the 'Come and See' portion of our study. It also offers a challenge to practice what we have learned." View the video segment "*Go and Do*: Review and a Challenge."

Reflect and Respond (5 minutes)

Ask the following questions to stimulate discussion:

- How do you understand the challenge presented in the video segment?
- What learnings did you write about in your study & reflection guide as you prepared for today's session? What connections

do you see between your learnings and the review of highlights presented in the video segment?

Plan Together (30 minutes)

Say: "During this session, we will plan together how we as a group will put into practice what we have learned about discernment. Our plan should reinforce what we have learned, set up future meetings so we can practice what we have learned, help us to learn more through our practice, and deepen our practice of being a faithful friend. We can use our next six weeks in many ways. We are the ones who will decide what we will do and when we will meet."

Explore Together

Discuss which aspects of the study of discernment your group wants to explore in the weeks ahead: discerning God's presence in our midst, discerning God's presence in our work, discerning God's presence in the shadows and the dark, discerning God's presence in the habit of our being. It is not necessary to choose one session only, but it may be helpful to learn which sessions had the most meaning for the group so that they might explore those topics more in-depth. Use this discussion as a way of working through a list of ideas.

List and Select Ideas

Invite the group to say what ideas they brainstormed and wrote in the boxes provided in Session 6 of their study & reflection guide (pages 60–61). Create a master list of their suggestions on a large sheet of paper, a chalkboard, or a whiteboard using the same idea prompts found in the boxes in the study & reflection guide. After you have listed all the group's ideas, give participants a marker and invite them to make a checkmark beside the five they like best. Ask them to consider the ideas in light of their discussion on the most meaningful topics. List the ones that receive the most checkmarks.

If you have more than five in the list, continue the process until it has been reduced to five ideas. You will use this list as a source for scheduling the next six weeks. *Be sure to include a closing worship and celebration for the final session.* (See ideas for this concluding worship and celebration in the "Additional Helps" section on pages 57–62 in this leader guide.)

Create a Schedule

Decide how many times and on what dates you will meet over the next six weeks. Some of your ideas may require meeting weekly. Other ideas may require another schedule. Meeting dates will be based upon the types of activities you choose to do. For example, a retreat may involve an overnight gathering. A mission experience could involve one day or several days. A book study might involve two or more weekly sessions. The point is to plan activities that you will do together in order to put into practice what you have learned. The schedule will emerge from the activities that you choose. Whatever your schedule, decide on dates and times. Record your plan on a calendar. Make sure that group members understand the meeting commitments they are making.

Designate Tasks

Will you need to make arrangements for speakers? Will you need to gather materials such as books, DVDs, or other resources? Will you need to make arrangements for a retreat or a field trip? Who will do such tasks? Who will be willing to serve on a worship and celebration team for the final meeting together? Make these decisions as a group and record them. Again, make sure that group members understand the commitments they are making.

Pray and Practice (5 minutes)

Practice for the "Go and Do" Portion of the Study

Thank the group for what they have contributed to the planning process for the weeks ahead. Encourage group members to do the following:

- Contact their faithful friend each week for coffee, lunch, a walk, or a phone conversation during the "Go and Do" portion of the study.
- Talk together about the plans the group has made and about the various activities they will experience as a group.
- Continue to use the questions in the "Faithful Friends" material in Session 1 of their study & reflection guide, "An Introduction to This Study Series" (pages 13–14), to stimulate their conversations.

Closing Prayer

Share prayer concerns. Invite participants to pray for their faithful friend and for the group this week and to pray for the meetings in the "Go and Do" portion of the study.

Close with a prayer asking God to support the group's plan for practicing discernment as a spiritual discipline in the weeks ahead. Pray that each participant will sense God's support and the encouragement of the group.

Additional Helps

Ideas for "Go and Do"

The idea prompts provided in the study & reflection guide for use in Session 6, "Planning the Next Steps Together" (pages 60–61), should generate many possibilities for what you might "go and do" together. If your group needs help responding to these idea prompts, you can suggest the following:

Lectio Divina Scripture Passages

Plan one or more sessions in which you will explore 1 Samuel 3:1–4:1. This is the story of God's call to Samuel and Samuel's response. After the group has practiced the Lectio Divina, invite them to discuss Samuel's attempts to discern what was happening to him. Talk also about how Samuel continued to discern God after his call, and what that might mean in the lives of group members.

Behavioral Changes to Make

Plan a group session that focuses on everyday ways and practices that can deepen your understanding of God's presence in your life and in the world. How can you heighten your ability to discern God's presence in all of life and how might you faithfully respond to God's presence with your actions? Invite a pastor or spiritual director to give you ideas and resources for cultivating discernment in your relationship with yourself, with God, and with others.

Ministry Events to Consider

Use a session to plan a strategy for sharing with your church how important it is to spend time and energy discerning God's presence in everyday life, in the world, at work, and during times of trouble. Ask your pastor and lay leadership to let you speak briefly at Sunday school, worship, other study groups about the deeply held early-church notion of "discerning God's presence." Go to these groups prepared with stationery cards and envelopes, and ask people to write a note to themselves about how they can develop ways to be closer in touch with God, to discern what God is doing, and to join God in that work. Later, send church members a postcard with Scripture and other quotes about discerning God in their midst, at work, in hard times, and in the world.

Mission Work to Conceive and Implement

Find out from people in your church, your community, or state if there are local groups that do work or projects that reflect attempts to discern God's desire for the world to be cared for, to be at peace, to be whole. If there are such groups, discuss possibilities for your group to be involved in their work.

Speakers to Invite

Invite a spiritual director or pastoral counselor to come and share her or his perspective on what it means to practice discerning God's presence in their midst. Ask them for suggestions or exercises you can do to prepare yourself to be an "active discerner" in your faith life.

You might invite someone from the Jewish or Islamic faith to speak to your group about discernment and how God is revealed in their religious tradition.

Field Trips, Retreats, Pilgrimages to Take

Sue Anne Steffey Morrow highlights Copake Village, part of the Camphill Foundation, which is dedicated to children, youth, and adults who have disabilities. Its mission statement is: "In a time where many are experiencing a crisis of spirit and search for meaning, Camphill offers a life of celebration, service, and community building in which all participants flourish."

Visit their website (*www.camphill.org*) to find out more about the organization. Camphill sponsors villages worldwide. Find out if one is close enough to visit. If so, contact them to arrange a visit. Contact them with questions about volunteering, finding a placement for a family member with disabilities, donating, or learning more about their programs. If you are unable to make a trip, there are DVDs available on the website.

Books to Read, Movies to See

Read one of the following books. Discuss how the book relates to the Christian trait of intimacy:

When the Heart Waits, by Sue Monk Kidd (Harper & Row, 1990), explores the journey and the mystery of growing spiritually and coming to live more in the habit of discerning God's presence and responding to it.

High Tide in Tucson, by Barbara Kingsolver (HarperCollins, 1995), is a collection of poignant essays about life and change. The title essay explores what it is that gentles us, grounds us, and challenges us to move on in our lives. It is a beautiful and provocative essay, ripe for discussion.

The Inner Voice of Love, by Henri J.M. Nouwen (Doubleday, 1996) is the "secret journal" Nouwen wrote during an extremely difficult time in his life. He had lost his self-esteem, his energy to work, and his hope in God. Reluctant for years to publish this journal, friends persuaded him to release it as the journey of one seeking new courage and hope to rejoin God in a deeper life of discernment.

The Joy of Full Surrender, by Jean-Pierre de Caussade (Paraclete, 1986), is a spiritual companion book for those who seek a practical way to find the reality of God in daily life. First published in France in 1861 as *Abandonment to Divine Providence*, it was an immediate success. The Reverend Jean-Pierre de Caussade died in 1751, but his first work, a classic, has gone through many editions and translations.

In the Shadow of God's Wings: Grace in the Midst of Depression, by Susan Gregg-Schroeder (Upper Room, 1997), is a courageous statement about living with chronic depression and discovering God's gifts in the midst of that life. A pastor at San Diego's First United Methodist Church, she describes discerning God in the middle of some very dark days. This book is a rare, true look at depression and spirituality.

Working: People Talk About What They Do All Day and How They Feel About What They Do, by Studs Terkel (New Press, 1997), is a collection of brief anecdotal stories of people reflecting on their lives at work. Though the first edition was published about thirty years ago, the stories and revelations are just as revealing and relevant today. The book is also available on DVD as the Broadway musical *Studs Terkel's Working* (Broadway Theater Archive, 1982).

Warm Springs (HBO Films, 2005) is a movie that tells the story of Franklin D. Roosevelt's time in Arkansas recuperating from adult onset polio. It tells of the people and presence that sustained him from the shadow world in which he sometimes lived to his nomination for the presidency of the United States. It is available at Amazon.com.

Live (Vanguard Records, 2002) is a collection of Mississippi John Hurt's music. Get a copy of the CD for one group session. Listen to "Monday Morning Blues," "Here I Am, O Lord, Send Me," and "Nearer My God to Thee." Listen to Hurt's music for his sense of wonder, his sense of God's presence in the world, and his understanding of God's presence in his work and life.

Other Ideas

Ask the group to think in the week ahead about watershed times in their lives, when they suddenly discerned some truth, some sense of God's presence. Ask them to come prepared to explore what it feels like to seek discernment, to ask God to make something known, and to receive (or not receive) a sense of God's presence in the process. Do they have family members or friends who actively seek discernment? Can they name historical figures or fictitious characters who exemplify what it means to discern God's presence in their lives and in the world?

A SAMPLE PLAN

Your group might plan a series of weekly meetings in which members would explore and practice discernment by reading *Fried Green Tomatoes at the Whistlestop Café,* by Fannie Flagg (Ballantine Books, 1987). It is the story of two women who manage to find God's presence through life's ups and downs in Alabama, from a menacing visit from a sheriff to the arrival of the Ku Klux Klan to the Great Depression. It challenges the reader to discern where God is and what God is doing through the lives of Flagg's two main characters. (If you like, you can view the movie *Fried Green Tomatoes* as a way to end your study of the book.)

If you choose this book study option, you might plan a series of sessions structured in a way similar to Sessions 2–5 in the "Come and See" portion of the study, using some or all of the following steps.

Welcome—Greet group members as they arrive.

Psalm and Silence—Choose the psalms you would like to pray.

Look and Listen—Read portions of the study book you choose.

Reflect and Respond—Discuss what you have read.

Lectio Divina—Select Scriptures on the subject of intimacy.

Pray and Practice—Make assignments for the next session and pray a closing prayer.

Encourage faithful friends to continue to contact one another and to talk about what the group has experienced together.

IDEAS FOR WORSHIP AND CELEBRATION

The final session of the study is a worship and celebration. The group who volunteered during Session 6, "Planning the Next Steps Together," will plan and implement this worship and celebration. Beginning with a meal is a good way to enjoy the friendships developed during this study of the Christian practice of attentiveness. Below are some suggestions to stimulate ideas. You may want to continue such practices as praying a psalm and lectio divina. You also may want to invite your pastor to serve Holy Communion during this worship and celebration. Be sure to make such arrangements ahead of time.

• Create a worship center.
• Share a meal.
• Pray a psalm.
• Sing hymns and praise choruses.
• Create a litany prayer of confession and assurance of God's forgiveness.
• Read the Bible.
• Share testimonies or faith stories.
• Make a commitment to God.
• Celebrate Holy Communion or a love feast.

.